What We Do at School

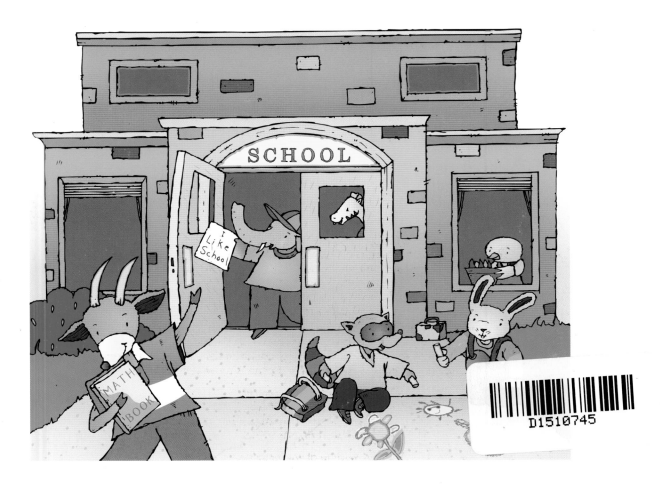

Written By **Alan Trussell-Cullen** · Illustrated By **Martin Lemelman**

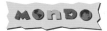

We like to read.

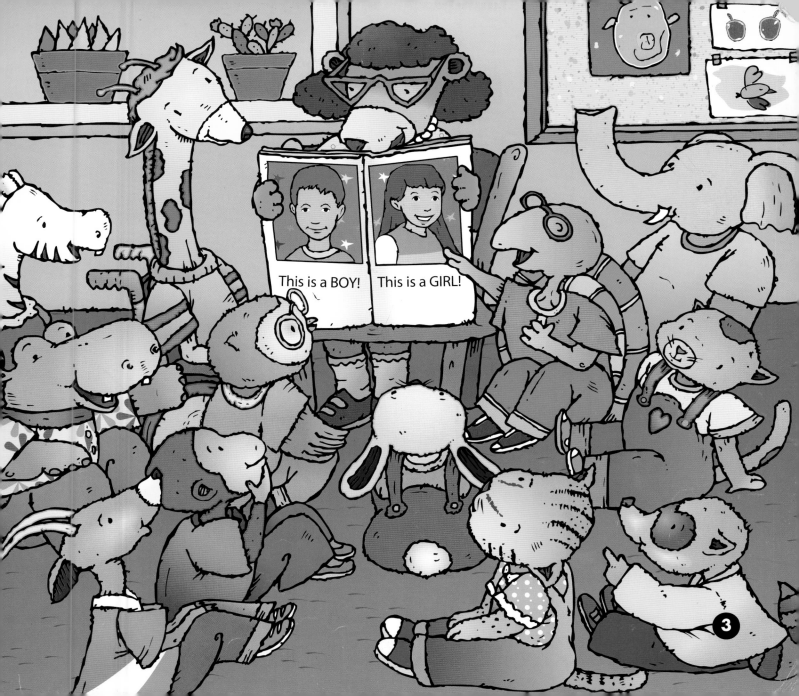

We like to count.

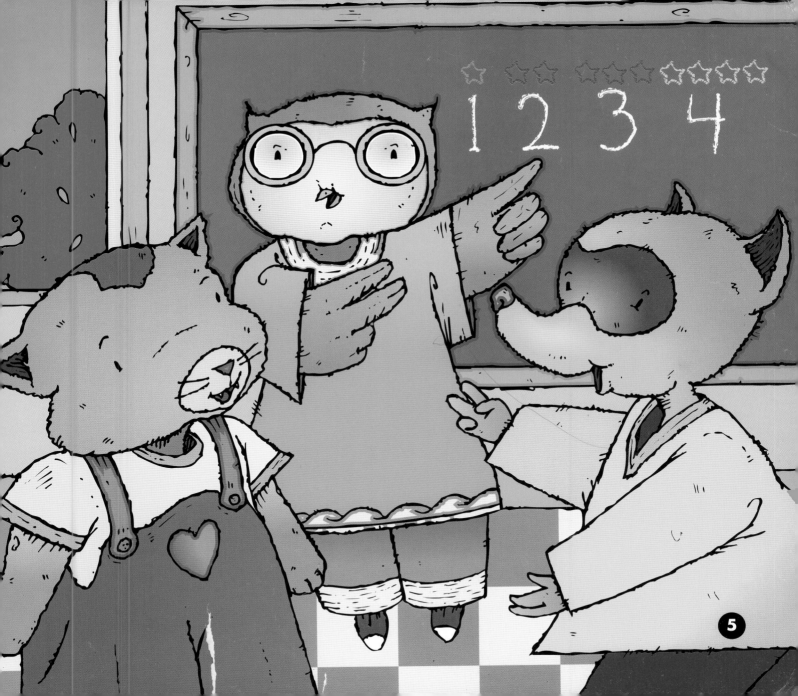

5

We like to sing.

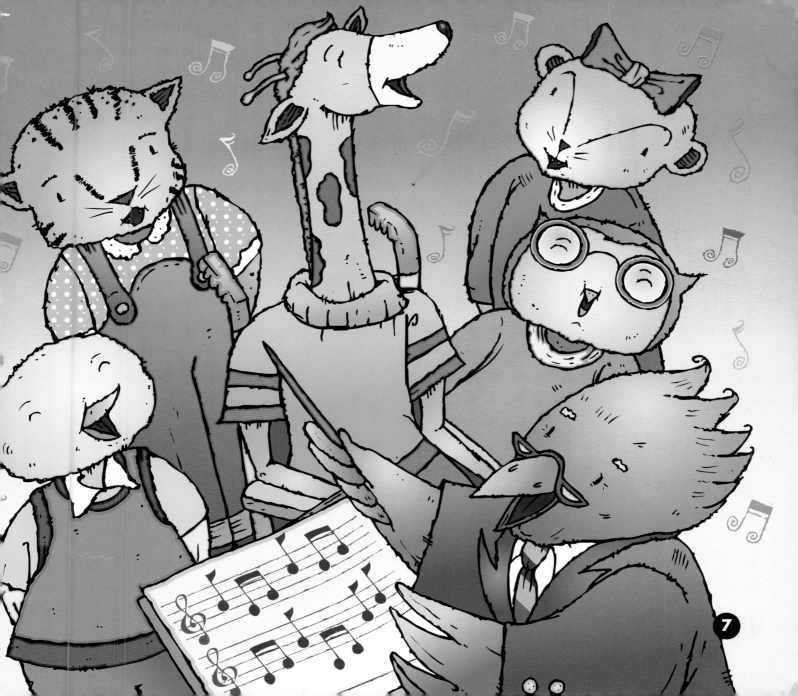

We like to write.

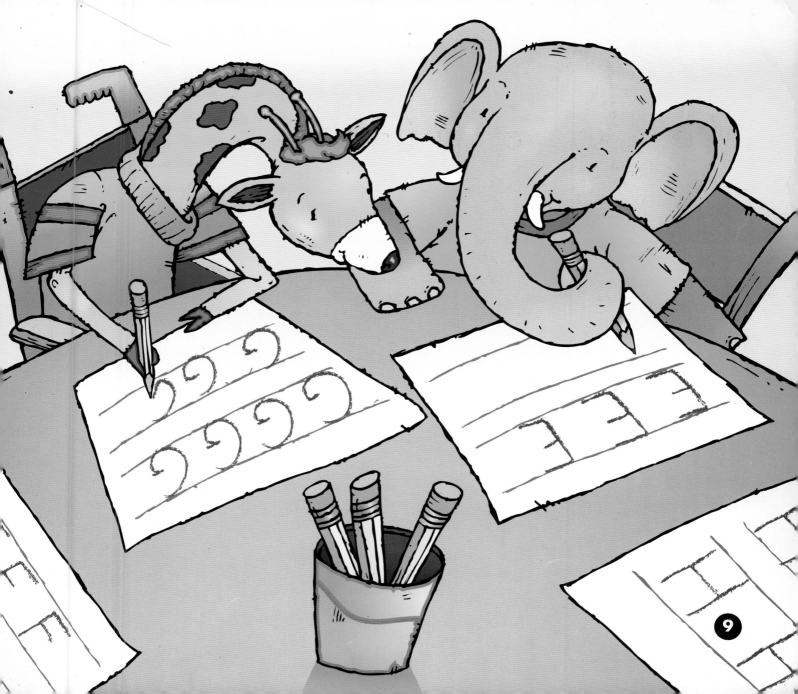

We like to run.

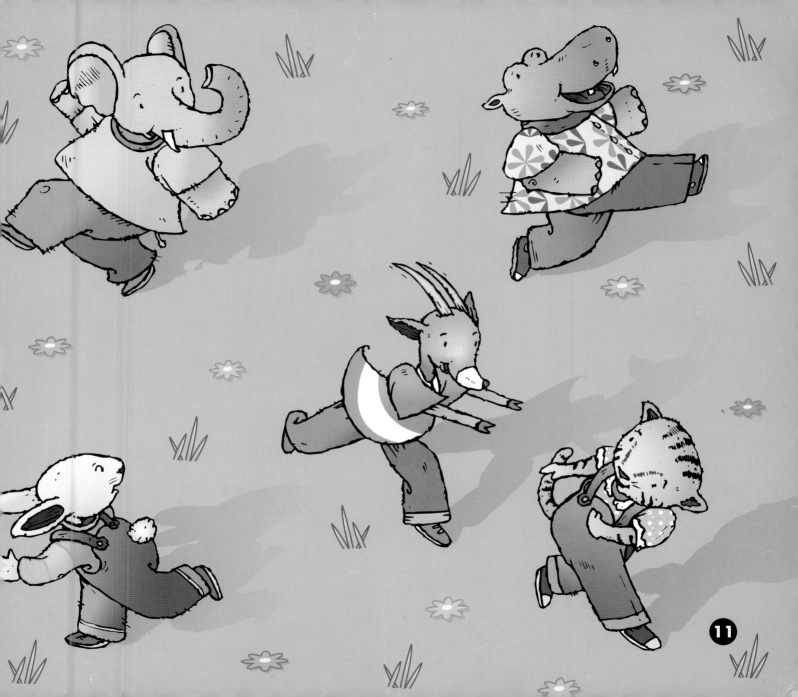

We like to swing.

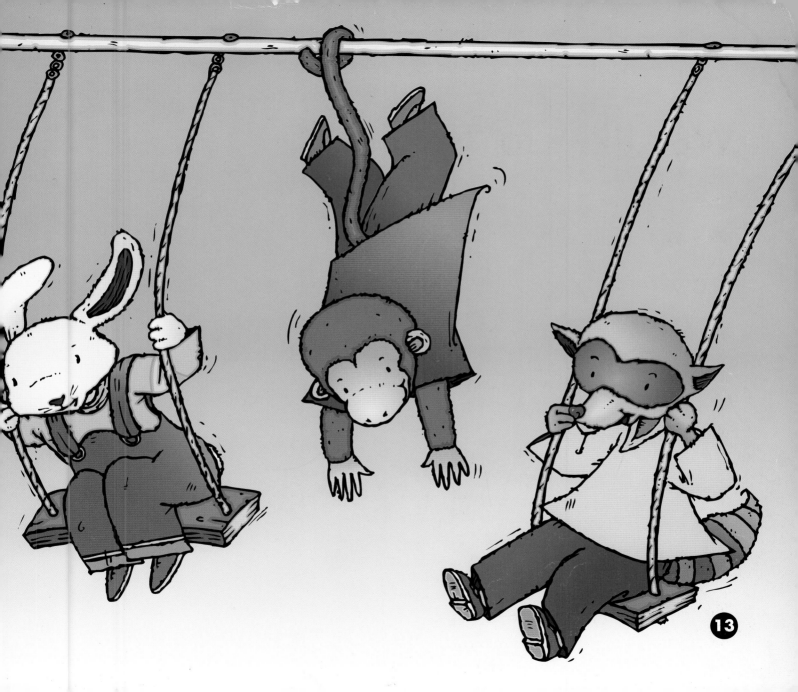

13

We like to eat.

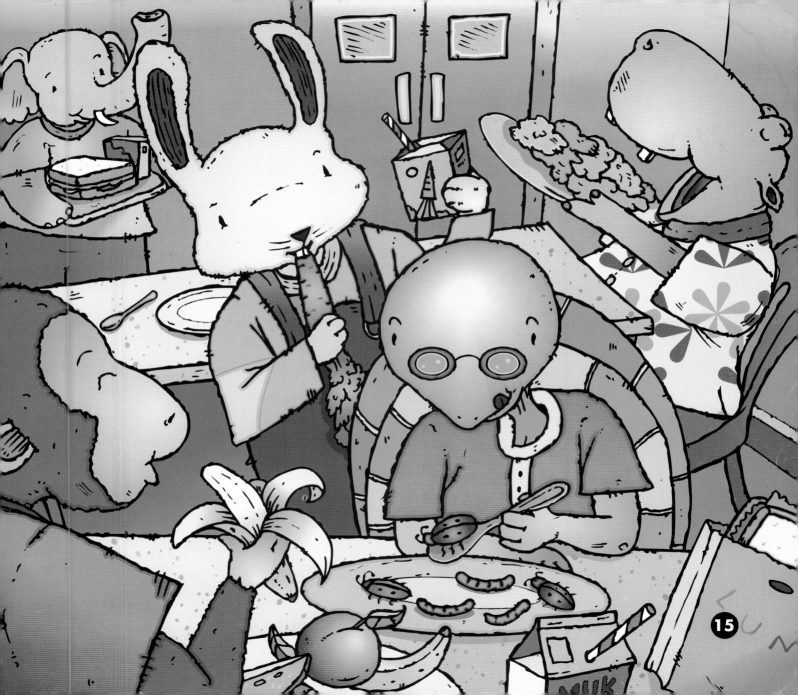

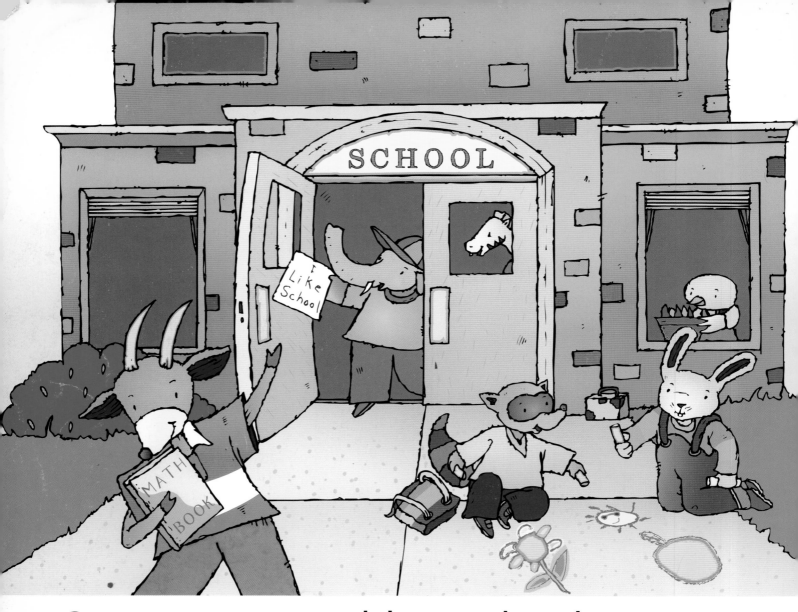

We like school!